VOCAL SELECTIONS

RODGERS AND HAMMERSTEIN™

Pipe Dream

Original Broadway Cast recording on RCA Victor Compact Disc and Cassette

Cover designed by Frank "Fraver" Verlizzo

ISBN 0-88188-602-5

HAL•LEONARD®
CORPORATION
7777 W. BLUEMOUND RD. P.O. BOX 13819 MILWAUKEE, WI 53213

EVERYBODY'S GOT A HOME BUT ME

Lyrics by OSCAR HAMMERSTEIN II
Music by RICHARD RODGERS

1. I rode by a house with the win-dows light-ed up Look-in'
(2. I) rode by a house where a poo-dle lay a-sleep In the

bright-er than a Christ-mas tree.___ And I
shad-ow of a wal-nut tree.___ And I

said to my-self as I rode by my-self, Ev-'ry
said to my-self as I rode by my-self, Ev-'ry

4

THE MAN I USED TO BE

Lyrics by OSCAR HAMMERSTEIN II
Music by RICHARD RODGERS

8

SUZY IS A GOOD THING

Lyrics by OSCAR HAMMERSTEIN II
Music by RICHARD RODGERS

If you walk with your eyes on the ground,

How can you tell where you're go - ing? Raise your eyes, take a good look a -

round, There are things to be learn - ing and know - ing, And the

ALL AT ONCE YOU LOVE HER

Lyrics by OSCAR HAMMERSTEIN II
Music by RICHARD RODGERS

you've scarce - ly met, But all at once you

love her. You like her eyes,

you tell her so. She thinks you're wise and

clev - er. You kiss good - night

THE NEXT TIME IT HAPPENS

Lyrics by OSCAR HAMMERSTEIN II
Music by RICHARD RODGERS

ALL KINDS OF PEOPLE

Lyrics by OSCAR HAMMERSTEIN II
Music by RICHARD RODGERS

buz - zard, He is some-thing I would nev-er like to be, But who knows what goes

on in his mind? He may think he is su-per-i-or to me._____ You

may not ad-mire ar-ma-dil-los, They're re-pul-sive and they lead pe-cul-iar lives. They

may not look at-trac-tive to you, But they're ver-y in-ter-est-ing to their wives._____

SWEET THURSDAY

Lyrics by OSCAR HAMMERSTEIN II
Music by RICHARD RODGERS

ALL KINDS OF PEOPLE • EVERYBODY'S GOT A HOME BUT ME
THE MAN I USED TO BE • SWEET THURSDAY • SUZY IS A GOOD THING
ALL AT ONCE YOU LOVE HER • THE NEXT TIME IT HAPPENS

RODGERS AND HAMMERSTEIN™

Pipe Dream

IS AVAILABLE FOR PERFORMANCE
BY YOUR ORGANIZATION,
WHETHER LARGE OR SMALL,
PROFESSIONAL OR AMATEUR,
NEWLY FORMED OR ESTABLISHED.

AND IT'S EASIER THAN YOU MIGHT THINK.
FOR OUR COMPLETE CATALOGUE
OF GREAT MUSICALS AVAILABLE
FOR PRODUCTION PLEASE CONTACT:

**RODGERS AND
HAMMERSTEIN
THEATRE LIBRARY™**

R&H

229 WEST 28 ST. — 11th FL.
NEW YORK , NY 10001

TELEPHONE: 212·564·4000
FACSIMILE: 212· 268·1245

WILLIAMSON MUSIC®

A RODGERS AND HAMMERSTEIN COMPANY

ISBN-13: 978-0-88188-602-3
Distributed By
HAL LEONARD
00312320   9 780881 886023

EXCLUSIVELY DISTRIBUTED BY

HAL•LEONARD®